Tithe and Tide

Tithe *and* Tide

DOROTHY RUFFIN

XULON PRESS

Xulon Press
2301 Lucien Way #415
Maitland, FL 32751
407.339.4217
www.xulonpress.com

© 2018 by Dorothy Ruffin

All rights reserved solely by the author. The author guarantees all contents are original and do not infringe upon the legal rights of any other person or work. No part of this book may be reproduced in any form without the permission of the author. The views expressed in this book are not necessarily those of the publisher.

Unless otherwise indicated, Scripture quotations taken from the King James Version (KJV)–*public domain*.

Printed in the United States of America.

ISBN-13: 978-1-54565-116-2

Dedications and Acknowledgments

I dedicate this book to my mother and to all who give God a chance to prove Himself to them. My mother trusted God and discovered that He is trustworthy. I acknowledge all the saints of God, who allow me to share their testimonies. As they obeyed His command in returning all the tithes and offerings to His storehouse, He manifested Himself to them with overflowing blessings. Awe-inspiring, He has opened the windows of heaven to pour out more blessings than they had room to receive, just as He said He would do. I extend my deepest gratitude to my friend and editor, Veronica McCullough. You have truly been an editorial Godsend. Your passion for clarity and enjoyment of the written language is amazing. Thank you for accepting the responsibility of making my book better in terms of excellence, transparency, accuracy, and value. God bless you abundantly for assisting me in bringing this book to pass. I would like to express my gratitude to my publishing team for their professionalism and assistance in the book publishing process. Thanks for making my dream come true. I praise my faithful God for being my Counselor, as I worship Him daily and observe His precious commands.

Table of Contents

Dedications and Acknowledgments v
Prologue. ix

Chapter 1: Can You Out-give God? 1
Chapter 2: You are Crazy 3
Chapter 3: Prove Me 9
Chapter 4: Things Last Longer 13
Chapter 5: Peace is Restored 17
Chapter 6: Are You a Robber? 21
Chapter 7: Testimonies 23
Chapter 8: A Book of Remembrance 29
Chapter 9: Biblical Study 31
Chapter 10: Scriptures to consider on this Study 37

References 39

Prologue

This book is for all who may need a little push and encouragement to know there is a God who is worthy of praise and cannot lie. I am a true witness, along with others, who have shared their encounters with the real and living God, who created heaven and earth. *Tithe and Tide* was birthed from heartfelt testimonies and my stories on how He confirmed His words; you will catch a glimpse of His promises coming to fruition. By His abundant provisions and grace, He rewards us in returning faithful tithes and offerings. I hope you will accept His promises and claim all that He has in store for those who trust Him and His infallible Word. This book provides scriptures for the readers on how to search His promises for themselves and do all He has commanded them to do. While obeying His command, you can watch how He demonstrates goodness to everyone courageous and patient enough to try Him and receive His promises. This happens when we release what is already His and seize the riches of His blessings that He has gathered for each one that loves and follows Him fully.

Unpopular though it may be, I must present you with the other side of the passage of scripture to assist you with a clear mind in making a wise decision in which way you should go.

Tithe and Tide

One may disobey and receive nothing but a broken cistern, or a pocket full of holes will lead the person to lose all of the goods he or she may have tried to own. Consequently, that would be considered a curse from God who wants to give you more. Never let anyone fool you into thinking that God is not a good God. He reveals to us how the enemy convinces millions of His people to trust in themselves to make ends meet instead of relying totally on Him. The enemy knows that God will open the windows of heaven to supply the believers more than enough to share with others, as they are led by His Spirit to go forth and convey His message of love. Let us pray, study His Word, and trust God for everything!

CHAPTER 1

Can You Out-give God?

When I was a child growing up, my sisters, brothers, and even my mother can attest to the fact that I am a giver. If you needed a nickel or a dime, I would give it to you. Well, I love contributing to others, and I knew God had given me this character trait. Someone may ask me, "Do you believe that God has given you this?" I believe that God has shown me in His Word that we all are sinners who need a Savior (Eph. 2:1-10, Rom. 3:23). Sinners, by nature, are selfish and look out for themselves, caring less about others. When the Spirit of the living God touches one's heart, it changes him or her into His likeness, and that includes giving.

So, can you out-give God? No! No one can out-give God. God gave His only begotten Son to show us how to live. God's Son Jesus came into this world as an infant, lived with us, and He willingly died for us (John 10:18). God raised His only begotten Son from the dead for us, who is making intercession for us in heaven even now and coming back for us soon (Acts 13:30-38, Rom. 8:34, John 14:1-3). Also, Jesus redeemed us from the sinfulness that we cannot overcome without His power.

We are to cheerfully return what He has asked us to His storehouse, so the holy men of God can proclaim the gospel of His only begotten Son Immanuel, the Anointed One. The storehouse is the temple or church (2 Chron. 31:4-12, Mal. 3:10, Matt. 21:12-13). As you see in Malachi 3:10, the LORD of hosts said to "Bring ye all the tithes into the storehouse, that there may be meat in Mine house," and the Lord went into the temple and said unto them, "It is written, My house shall be called the house of prayer, but ye have made it a den of thieves." Both the Old and New Testament declare what the Lord's house is. What is next? Before you can offer to someone who has asked you to give, you should have a report of that particular person to determine if he or she can be trusted. This book is filled with testimonies of real people who have tested God and realized He is a faithful and loving God to every word that He has spoken about giving tithes and offerings. Returning tithes and offerings will support those who have been chosen to spread the good news of His precious Son to all nations. When this solemn work is finished, this same God will send His dear Son in the clouds to accompany His faithful children home to heaven to enjoy eternal life with Him.

CHAPTER 2

You are Crazy

Raised as a Baptist, I was taught by my mother how God loved me through His precious Son, Jesus. Later, I found so many wonderful things in God's Word that He wanted me to do. Things I did not know until I searched the Scriptures. One of the precious truths I learned was the biblical Sabbath, which is not on Sunday, the first day of the week but on Saturday, the seventh day of the week (Exod. 20:8-11). Soon after, as I was obeying Him regarding the real Sabbath day, I even asked my former Baptist pastor about this precious truth, and he said, "Yes, the biblical Sabbath was on Saturday and not Sunday." With the excitement of this new truth from the Word of God, I asked my pastor why he did not keep it on the day as God had said. His reply was, "Because I was raised that way." I asked him, "If you were raised stealing, would you continue to steal?" He dropped his head and walked away and never said another word to me. I knew then it was the influence of God's Spirit using me at the early age of 19 to witness powerfully. Sad to say, this pastor never went back to his congregation to proclaim that precious truth. Actually, my mother arranged that encounter with my former Baptist pastor. She thought I had gotten into an occult after joining the Seventh-day Adventist Church that adheres to the Lord's true Sabbath on Saturday.

Still, while learning more and more about what God wanted me to do in keeping His Sabbath, I came to an awareness of returning tithes and offerings in His Word. I began to tithe at the age of 19 and joyfully abided by what He required me to give. As I gave what belonged to Him, my mother called me crazy. "You are crazy," she said to me, for giving so much of my money to that church. Immediately, I bowed on my knees and prayed for my mother with love in my heart. I asked God to show her that what I was doing was not crazy but instead to teach her what He expected all of His children to do, return His tithes and offerings.

I got married, and my mother was happy for me. Still, she thought that I was irrational for returning tithes and offerings. Nevertheless, God kept our loving relationship as mother and daughter intact. For seven years, my mother considered me weird for obeying what the Lord had instructed me to do. One day, I received a phone call from her. On the other end of the phone, I heard my mother's voice sounding as if she were somewhat disappointed in something she had done. She calmly said, with a compassionate tone, "Dottie, I am sorry for calling you crazy." I did not instantly understand what she was talking about until she explained. She started by saying, "I just talked to a lady on the phone, and I told her I needed prayer for my financial difficulties, and she asked me if I returned tithes and offerings. I replied that I was on a fixed income, and the woman said to me that it did not matter if I were on a fixed income, but I should still return tithes and offerings regardless." Then, she explained to my mother this biblical truth was found in Malachi 3:7-18. I was so happy she realized I was not crazy for tithing, and that God's Word was all I observed. My mother began returning her tithes and offerings from that day forward.

Being tithers, my mother and I were getting closer than ever. I know the Lord was smiling upon us both because blessings were being displayed in our lives. While living in a world where the famous are always looked upon as a blessing to others, it can bring a smile to your face if someone tells you that you resemble a famous person. Well, that is just what happened to me. Some time ago, my mother and I went on a job to help clean Housing Urban Development (HUD) homes in Marrero, Louisiana. Many families were evicted from their homes. I must confess in some of the homes we entered, it was a somber sight. It was as if someone punched holes in some of the walls out of frustration. The unkempt homes were so unattractive, and they were vandalized, too. Numerous ones were simply a mess to clean, so it was not an easy task to do. Nevertheless, my mother and I cleaned the homes and praised God for His goodness.

We wandered down memory lane about the very first time I started returning my tithes and offerings. After conversion, I realized that God wanted me to return 10 percent of my income, along with an offering. I studied this from His Word in Malachi 3, and low and behold, I was filled with His Spirit after reading this and embarked on returning it with gladness. My husband and the father of my children, at that time, offered my mother and me a job cleaning houses to supply a little money in our pockets and also to assist him. This was a side job to help our family financially. On this particular day of praise, I had to take my little girl to one of the houses my mother and I were to clean. Praise God this house was not as badly in need of cleaning as some others had been. My mother and I began to praise the Lord God for all His goodness. We recalled how we never had been without what we needed since we were obeying His master plan of returning tithes and offerings. It was also wonderful that we had my first-born daughter Kimberly with us. She was 3 at the time and very obedient to our instructions as we were cleaning the house. What a blessing God bestowed on us all! Working diligently, we noticed that the house appeared cleaner, for some reason, much faster that day; it took less time than the other houses.

We packed all our cleaning materials and headed back home. Before I could go home, my mother and I realized we had to stop for some items to wash clothes and make dinner for my family. We shopped in a supermarket in Marrero, Louisiana, and browsed for the lowest cost of washing powder. While in the aisle, my little daughter tugged at me because she needed to use the restroom. I started to become a bit frustrated because I hated to use public restrooms; it was a ritual which I did not like. I would take some toilet paper, line the toilet seat, and hold her up in my arms, and then let her do what she needed to do, all along trying my best to not let her sit or touch the toilet seat. Well, she kept on complaining to me while my mother and I were looking for the cheapest washing powder to buy. I had only about $7 and some change to purchase detergent, a pack of red beans, and one pound of rice. My mother said to me with a soft voice, "Dottie, go take Kimberly to the restroom. I will look for the cheapest washing powder for you." So, I headed straight to the restroom.

As I finished my ritual with Kimberly, I left the stall and went to wash my little girl's hands and my hands when a well-dressed lady entered the restroom, looked at me, and said: "You look like Whitney Houston!" I was flattered because I always admired Whitney Houston and have always felt she was very beautiful. What a great feeling to hear those complimentary words! That same lady looked at me and said she was a representative for the Tide Detergent Company and asked me if I would like some commercial boxes of Tide. Without delay, I replied, yes. I waited until she finished taking care of her business and walked out of that restroom with her. I went to my mother and shared the good news with her. Believe it or not, that was the best washing powder I used and is still one of the best on the market today. God had shown up and out for me again. That lady had given me five huge commercial boxes of Tide. Look at my God how He showed up for me!

God opened the windows of heaven and poured me a blessing that there was not room enough to receive it. I handed one box of Tide to my mother, kept two for myself, and shared the rest with friends. Unable to use it all, I had to share, just as God had said in His Word. I no longer needed to buy the cheapest washing powder that day, not at all. God blessed me with the best on the market. This encounter represented one of those "aha" moments for the title of my book, *Tithe and Tide*. He had given this to me when my little girl, Kimberly, was 3, now grown, and married to a fine Christian man, who is the father of my three precious granddaughters: Naomi, Faith, and Hannah. I thank God for my family. The tithes and offerings were returned first, and then the abundance of "tide" emerged.

One of my favorite scriptures is Romans 8:28, and I have experienced this in so many ways. The very first time I realized this verse became apparent in my life was at the supermarket. God brought to my mind this fact that if my little girl did not need to go to the restroom, I would have never met the lady who was Tide's representative. Therefore, I would not have received the blessings of the Lord that day. I started out frustrated, but God turned my frustration into an overflowing blessing. At an early age, when my child was growing up, I learned this lesson. Romans 8:28: "And we know that all things work together for good to them that love God, to them who are the called according to His purpose." My faith and my mother's faith grew from this experience.

CHAPTER 3

Prove Me

As the years passed, God asked me to test Him again. After a life of obedience to the Word of God in returning tithes and offerings, I was confronted with another test from my Creator. My husband lost his job, so I was the only one working in December. You all know this was a stressful time where everyone was purchasing gifts for others in remembrance of Christ, my Lord's birth. Children and even adults are affected by this festive time.

Sadly, some children and adults have been affected in a negative way, and some in a positive way. Thoughts of suicide are prevalent during these days in remembrance of His birth. Nevertheless, it should be a time of hope and love because of such an awesome event recorded in the Gospel of Christ Jesus, our Lord (Luke 1-2). No one knew my husband had lost his job, except God, him, and me. This was a tough financial time because the rent was due, I had to pay for family gifts, and obtain a $10 gift for one of my choir members. You see, we had exchanged names to buy one another a gift for the memories of the time we spent together during the year. Also, we were grateful to God for giving us a successful year in praising Him in the church choir ministry.

Furthermore, I was a believer of all God had done in the past when it came to paying rent or returning what belonged to God through tithes and offerings, so this was a no-brainer. My husband told me we had to pay rent, and my reply was, "Honey, we have to obey God and trust Him. We must return a faithful tithe and offering, which is 10 percent of our income and a generous offering of 5 percent, making a total of 15 percent." My husband looked at me and said, "Ok, Dot." I smiled and prepared the tithes and offerings in an envelope that our church had provided for these special and sacred funds. We both went to the renter's office and talked to the manager about the rent. We explained to her the situation about my husband's unemployment and informed her that we did not have the rent at this time. Boldly, we conveyed that it will be paid at a later date. Since we always paid promptly, she understood with a compassionate attitude. By faith we perceived His power working through her to respond in the way that she did.

Happily, we left the renter's office praising God for helping us in our serious dilemma. On Sabbath, getting ready to attend church was a joy. As I sat there in the church, the basket was passed for the tithes and offerings. Joy filled my heart to return to God as He had asked me to in Malachi 3:10. I took the envelope for my family's tithes and offerings and merrily dropped it in the basket, feeling inside that the Lord was going to work everything out for my family and me. From that time on, I was elated to be obedient to my God. We worshipped Him through obedience; what joy filled our hearts that day!

After attending church at sunset, our choir members planned a social gathering with all their families and friends. Weeks before, we pulled a name from a bag to exchange gifts at our social event. Yes, even though my husband and I did not have enough money, God inspired me to get that $10 gift for my special friend. Walking by faith, I bought it with joy in my heart. Arriving at the social gathering, I must admit this was the most heartwarming time to be together with friends and family. We had delicious food and a host of good friends and family, too. Surely, the LORD of hosts had opened the windows of heaven way before my husband and I had realized it. Before we returned our tithes and offerings, God already planned to shower a blessing upon us.

My husband, the director of our choir, became aware that the president of the choir organized a special honor for him. She presented him with an envelope and conveyed gratitude for his tireless commitment in directing the choir all year. My husband expressed appreciation for the choir members and forwarded me the envelope. Excitedly, I laid it in my purse and continued to enjoy the gathering with our friends and family.

When the social gathering was over, everyone said their goodbyes. Driving away, I regarded the event as one of the best times with friends and family. The gift I received was wonderful, too. My husband asked me to open the envelope that was presented to him at the gathering. I unsealed it, and to our surprise, it was cash! It was about $750. Our rent was $590. Cheerfully, we were overwhelmed with praises to God for proving Himself before we returned tithes and offerings. As a matter of fact, I still get teary-eyed about the numerous ways that He performs

His promises. The faithful God that I love and serve is a promise keeper. He is worthy of all my praise and obedience to His Word. Proven to be trustworthy, He is God all by Himself because there are no limits to what He has said over and over again if we trust Him. We should endeavor to trust Him more.

CHAPTER 4

Things Last Longer

I remember the times when things lasted longer, and in many ways, they still do. Entrusting to God all things that He already possesses causes them to endure by His grace. All our material belongings—shoes, clothes, appliances, homes, and cars last longer. Even I am surprised to have appliances that last longer when I return my tithes and offerings to Him. Still, I can personally attest to the fact of how God has taken care of my shoes to the point where they do not wear out and look as if they are new. My heart is pleased because the Lord has proved to me that He can be trusted, even when I encounter obstacles in life. The joy of returning tithes and offerings has given me such hope in knowing God's love will be extended. Preachers and teachers enter God's house to preach and teach His Word, bringing millions to Him before He returns to take us home.

    The LORD of hosts says in Malachi 3:10-12: "Bring ye all the tithes into the storehouse, that there may be meat in mine house, and prove me now herewith, saith the LORD of hosts, if I will not open you the windows of heaven, and pour you out a blessing, that there shall not be room enough to receive it.

And I will rebuke the devourer for your sakes, and he shall not destroy the fruits of your ground; neither shall your vine cast her fruit before the time in the field, saith the LORD of hosts. And all nations shall call you blessed: for ye shall be a delightsome land, saith the LORD of hosts." The meat is His Word, and the storehouse is His sanctuary, which is His house of prayer (John 4:34; Matt. 4:4). The devourer is Satan, that old devil. In I Peter 5:8, it says, "Be sober, be vigilant; because of your adversary the devil, as a roaring lion, walketh about, seeking whom he may devour." Satan plants this idea in your mind that if you hold onto what already belongs to the LORD of hosts, you will profit more. What he is really trying to do is devour you, even as the LORD of hosts has warned you about his schemes. The LORD is going to "rebuke the devourer for your sakes" (Mal. 3:11). He is referring to His church as a whole. You see, in Hebrew, the words "ye, you, and your" are plural. Therefore, when the LORD states, "ye, you, and your," He is communicating to His children as a whole, not individually. After all, He encourages the church to cooperate with Him, so He can distribute His money to spread the good news to everyone in the world. What a commission of love the church has to fulfill! This good news is a love message that focuses on Jesus's resurrection and how He redeemed us from the curse of sin. If we, as a church, give what He has commanded, there will be no shortage in His storehouse.

A servant of the Lord, Ellen G. White, wrote this in her book, *Acts of Apostles* (AA):

> As God's work extends, calls for help will come more and more frequently. That these calls may

be answered, Christians should heed the command, "Bring ye all the tithes into the storehouse, that there may be meat in Mine house" (Mal. 3:10). If professing Christians would faithfully bring to God their tithes and offerings, His treasury would be full. There would then be no occasion to resort to fairs, lotteries, or parties of pleasure to secure funds for the support of the gospel.

Men are tempted to use their means in self-indulgence, in the gratification of appetite, in personal adornment, or in the embellishment of their homes. For these objects many church members do not hesitate to spend freely and even extravagantly. But when asked to give to the Lord's treasury, to carry forward His work in the earth, they demur. Perhaps, feeling that they cannot well do otherwise, they dole out a sum far smaller than they often spend for needless indulgence. They manifest no real love for Christ's service, no earnest interest in the salvation of souls. What marvel that the Christian life of such ones is but a dwarfed, sickly existences!

He whose heart is aglow with the love of Christ will regard it as not only a duty, but a pleasure, to aid in the advancement of the highest, holiest work committed to man–the work of presenting to the world the riches of goodness, mercy, and truth (338).

Most people believe that God sends only financial breakthroughs, but He also sends various blessings that you may need at that specific time in your life.

CHAPTER 5

Peace is Restored

Do you remember the content in Chapter 4, Things Last Longer? God's blessings come in different ways, particular to each individual's needs. They are tailor-made for anyone who obeys. In the past, I almost had a nervous breakdown but God! He stepped in and bestowed upon me the blessings of His peace that no human being could have given me. His tender care and mighty hand sustained me. My physical health is intact; also, I am whole mentally, spiritually, and emotionally.

After raising my two beautiful daughters, Kimberly and Dionne, God blessed me to further my education. Happily, I graduated with an extremely high GPA. This goal was only possible by prayer and His grace. During my studies each day, He encouraged and strengthened me to study effectively to earn the grades that I received. Once I completed my undergraduate studies, I purchased my first car without any credit. The Holy Spirit instructed me to bring a copy of my undergraduate degree with me to the Nissan car dealership. I obeyed. Arriving at Nissan, I informed them that I received my undergraduate degree from Portland State University. They immediately assisted me in acquiring the car that I desired.

Furthermore, they inquired about my employment. I was serving at a Christian Academy as the lead teacher working with three to four-year-old children. Praise the Lord, I was approved for my dream car. I believe my degree set the stage for an opening in obtaining the vehicle. It was a black Nissan Versa Sedan with a sunroof; a fine-looking car, which I still own.

Later, while working at the Christian Academy, it was not easy because of insufficient income. Consequently, it was challenging to keep up with all of my needs and expenses. Early that morning before starting my day, I had daily Bible meditation and prayer. I shared my concern with God about after returning my tithes and offerings that month, I would not have enough to service my car. Well, after saying, "Amen," I felt in my spirit His reassurance that it will be alright because He will provide for me. Filled with so much peace, I forgot I had even asked Him about the servicing of my car.

I was scheduled to be at the academy at 6:30 a.m. to welcome the parents and children. Upon arriving at the Academy, I greeted the children and some of the parents. I served the children breakfast before class started. During breakfast, there is always singing and smiling with the children. The children loved the singing and enjoyable interaction, as they waited for food, and while they were eating their breakfast each day.

God had manifested Himself that morning concerning my car service when one of my students' parents walked in and greeted me with a hug, as always. The parent stated she had something to give me, but she had to go back to the car to get it.

She came back and handed me a crisp $100 bill. She explained that something motivated her to give the $100 to me last week, but she forgot. However, as she showered, something reminded her not to fail to remember it and to give it to me that morning. Tears began to swell in my eyes. I thanked her with a tight hug and commented that I really needed it.

Right away, she remarked someone had given the $100 to her, and something prompted her to give it to me. Besides, she indicated she did not need it. When she left, I turned from the children, who saw my eyes filled with tears, and as I swung around, the Holy Spirit whispered to me, saying, "That something was Me." Through His infinite mercy, He prepared a way for me to provide proper car maintenance. I will never forget that morning of His bountiful blessing. With tears of joy, I expressed gratitude to Him for answering my prayers. God is real! Yes, He is.

CHAPTER 6

Are You a Robber?

Imagine that someone gives you $100 and instructs you to only accept it if you give at least 10 percent and a thanks offering. The purpose of the requirement is to prove that you appreciate the gift, but instead, you take all the money and deceive the person by saying, "Okay, I will." Running away, you do what you want to do with the money, and you do not keep your promise.

Furthermore, days and weeks go by, and you do not even call or talk to that person again. Are you a robber or a liar? Yes, you robbed and lied to the giver because you agreed to pay what he or she asked you to give. Well, the Bible says that everything belongs to God (Gen. 1:1; Deut. 10:14; 1 Chron. 29:10-14; Ps. 24:1). He has given us the money we have, and He has asked you and me to return 10 percent and a sacrificial offering as a cheerful supporter. Neglecting to obey His command, we become robbers and liars. The Bible declares that when a person does not return tithes and offerings, he or she will be cursed (Mal. 3:9). If husbands and wives have robbed God's storehouse, their household will be cursed, knowing that each one is robbing God. It is like realizing big holes are in your pocket but still putting all your money in it. Does that make sense? No! Don't you agree?

Sadly, many pastors and teachers do not like to give the people of God the whole story when it comes to telling them that they "are cursed with a curse" when withholding tithes and offerings (Mal. 3:9). That is a double curse! This truth will help you and me to make a wise decision to obey God and ignore the devil's trickery. He frequently persuades people to hold onto their money, and they will be fine. All along, he knows that money belongs to God. I have been inspired to share this precious truth to all of God's children everywhere in the world. Remember that the devil is behind all disobedience to God.

Let us gird ourselves and put on the whole armor of God and fight the good fight of faith and prove God's strength, righteousness, and mercy. He will do what He says He will do. I tried Him for myself, and He is a faithful and loving God. He will do for you just as He has done for all who have made up their minds to trust and obey Him. There are blessings from heaven's windows waiting for you. May God pour out His abundant blessings on you today as you serve and obey Him by bringing tithes and offerings to His storehouse. Have you received the blessing that is waiting to be poured from the windows of heaven for you? Remember, "The earth is the LORD'S, and the fullness thereof; the world, and they that dwell therein" (Ps. 24:1).

CHAPTER 7

Testimonies

Testimony 1

Trial and Error

This first testimony in this book is from a lady who prefers to stay anonymous; however, she wanted to share her story to help others avoid the mistakes she made in the past.

"I have been returning faithful tithes and offerings for years and have watched the Lord fulfill His promises. Nevertheless, I failed in keeping my trust in Him as the years passed by. I was praising the Lord for all He had given me, and low and behold, I found myself relying on my ability. Taking the wheel from the Lord, I drove down the road of using the tithes and offerings because I was in a bind. I felt helpless! I began to take God's money and paid my bills. Well, at first, I believed it was working, and every time I said to myself, 'I will give my tithes and offerings back to God when I get my next check.'

The next month rolled around, and I was in more debt than when I started. I owed more and more to God, and still, I had gotten behind in my bills worse than the beginning. I cried out to the Lord, and He heard my cry. I was raised from that deep pit that I had allowed myself to get into and now realized that God must be first when I get my check. I now take His 10 percent and an offering out first, pay my bills, and I have been blessed by Him. Yes, I know for sure that if I put His money aside first, He will open heaven's windows for me. My God opened others' hearts to give to me in my time of need. Some of the people who have given me money would say to me, 'God led me to give this to you.' The windows of heaven are open for me!!!"

Testimony 2

Double Tithing

"My name is Ann Assent, and it's an honor to share my Christian testimony. My husband and I have not seen bills that have not been paid because we double tithe. We both have not missed a meal. When we send a card out to someone, we always have a little something in it to give. We always take the tithes out first before anything else. We have never seen the Lord forsake us. You can't beat God's giving."

Testimony 3

Literature Evangelist

"My name is Patsy Arthur and being a literature evangelist, I would return my tithes and offerings. When I was taking care of my late brother, I did not have much of my own; however, I would always return tithes and offerings. I was a vegetarian, and my brother was not. However, he became one, and he began to get better. Nevertheless, he turned and began to eat flesh food later. Taking care of my brother alone was very stressful. Therefore, I had to take medication, one tablet for stress. I did not have much money when I was taking care of my brother.

After my ex-husband died, I found out that I could get some of his social security, and that helped me. One day, a brown envelope came in the mail. What was in it? My late brother was ill with cancer at the time, and the check in that envelope was written out to me, Patsy Arthur. 'Lord,' I said. I had an appointment with the doctor later that day, and my doctor said, 'Pat, why is your blood pressure so high?' I told him I had gotten something that will help me out financially, and he said I had to calm down. I was so excited that he kept me there until my blood pressure went down. You see, when my brother was sick, I assisted in maintaining the records to report to the lawyers in how I spent his money, which did not include me in the spending per se. I sent every month the report to the lawyers, and this was very stressful for me. God always provided for me here and there.

I said with excitement about the check that I had to get my tithes and offerings out of this money. Even when I get into a tight situation, something always comes in the mail. God always sent me something. One day, I received $500 from my niece and another $100 from someone else. God always opened my niece's heart to me, as she always sent me money to lighten my load. I even found $80 under my phone, and to this day, I do not know how it was placed there. Any gift that God provides me with, I always return a faithful tithe and offering to Him. Again, I can say, 'God always provides!'"

Testimony 4

I Love the Song

"I love the song, 'You can't beat God's giving, no matter how you try.' By His grace, my husband and I give monthly tithes and offerings from our salaries and other financial blessings that we receive. We don't realize that giving what God requires is our service to Him. Returning our tithes and offerings is just one way to honor God and express gratitude for His provisions.

I'm sharing my testimony to encourage someone to trust God and watch how He will show up and show out. A couple of months ago, we had additional financial obligations, so after we paid our tithes and offerings, we didn't have enough left to cover all the debts. Unexpectedly, God blessed my husband with another source of income the next week. That source of income was just on time and provided for the rest of our obligations, with some leftover. You see, God is always on time and will come through when we need it the most.

If you withhold what belongs to Him, you limit your blessings. However, if you are a cheerful tither, He will fill your cup to run over with the blessings that He has waiting for you. David writes, 'Thou preparest a table before me in the presence of my enemies: thou anointest my head with oil; my cup runneth over'

(Ps. 23:5). What does the cup symbolize? It speaks of God's blessings and provisions. The cup is our daily portion in life that God gives each man and woman as He desires. He keeps our cup running over for us to share the blessings with others. Think about it: as we faithfully give to Him, our cups are always overflowing. Expect His Abundant Blessings."

Veronica McCullough

CHAPTER 8

A Book of Remembrance

People forget what you have done for them or spoken on their behalf, but that's not God. He has a book of remembrance about you that contains everything you have said He has done for you, and you have done in His name. Oh yes, He does. Living in a world where people soon fail to remember the kind things you have done and have said about them is startling. Nevertheless, God keeps good records of what you and I have spoken about Him. He listens attentively; He cares and is pleased with us when we talk about His gracious love and kindness. Mostly, He basks in our conversations about His faithfulness to every promise that is written in His Holy Word, which is the Holy Bible.

Now, let us reflect on what Malachi 3:16 says to confirm this fact: "Then they that feared the LORD spake often one to another: and the LORD hearkened, and heard it, and a book of remembrance was written before Him for them that feared the LORD, and that thought upon His name." Who do you believe is writing those things? Every time we earnestly fear Him in loving obedience, He writes down what we convey about Him.

Tithe and Tide

Not only does He keep good records by having a book of remembrance with our names in it and of the things we praised Him for doing, but also, He gives us the ability to discern right from wrong during our lifetime here on earth.

Isn't that amazing that the God of the universe takes time to jot down things you shared with others concerning Him? What a blessing! The book of remembrance illustrates how God delights in us when we render service to Him. This is so important to Him that He inspires His faithful ones that their love and service for Him is appreciated. During Christ's second coming, He will reward them for their deeds of love.

Moreover, we, as His children, should hold fast to His example and write things down that He has done for us and meditate on them. In the days to come, we can remind ourselves how He has brought us through the storms of life. Communing with Him daily through prayer and by studying The Word will bring glory, honor, and happiness to our God. He is pleased with us when His love shines through our lives as a testimony to everyone.

This would cause us to glide through and above the darkest clouds of any situation that seems to zap the life out of us. During our most difficult times and lack of faith, we can declare He has been there all the way, with us all the time, as we contemplate and read what we have written in our memoirs about Him.

CHAPTER 9

Biblical Study

Malachi 3:7-18

Millions have been blessed by returning to God what belongs to Him. Now, we will explore Malachi 3:7-18 about making an intelligent decision to be blessed, and not cursed, because of unbelief or disobedience.

Verse 7: "Even from the days of your fathers ye are gone away from Mine ordinances, and have not kept them. Return unto Me, and I will return unto you, saith the LORD of hosts. But ye said, Wherein shall we return?"

The LORD of hosts has made a promise that if we return to Him, He will return unto us. Our forefathers have been disobedient by not doing what the LORD of hosts required them to do. They did not follow His ordinances. When we repent and return to the LORD of hosts, He will return unto us. Zechariah 1:3 says, "Therefore say thou unto them, Thus saith the LORD of hosts; Turn ye unto Me, saith the LORD of hosts, and I will turn unto you, saith the LORD of hosts." The last statement in Malachi verse 7 is shown as a question, "But ye said, Wherein shall we return?"

The answer comes loud and clear in the form of a question in verse 8.

Verse 8: "Will a man rob God? Yet ye have robbed Me. But ye say, Wherein have we robbed Thee? In tithes and offerings."

Tithes and offerings belong to the LORD of hosts! Those who refuse to abide by the law of the tithe are robbers in the sight of God. Have you ever considered yourself a robber? If we do not pay back what is His, the blessings of the gospel are hindered. In other words, the gospel is shared with many from our tithes, so when we withhold them, we deny others from receiving the gospel. What a serious charge against those who have robbed God's storehouse by holding onto His tithes and offerings!

Verse 9: "Ye are cursed with a curse: for ye have robbed Me, even this whole nation."

Some may say to themselves, "Is God speaking only to the church members and not the priests and the pastors?" The LORD of hosts is not excluding the priests; He informs them that if they do not hear Him and will not take it to heart to give glory to His name, He will send a curse. Their blessings will be cursed, too.

Malachi 2:1-2, "And now, O ye priests, this commandment is for you. If ye will not hear, and if ye will not lay it to heart, to give glory unto My name, saith the LORD of hosts, I will even send a curse upon you, and I will curse your blessings: yea, I have cursed them already, because ye do not lay it to heart."

Verse 10: "Bring ye all the tithes into the storehouse, that there may be meat in Mine house, and prove Me now herewith, saith the LORD of hosts, if I will not open you the windows of heaven, and pour you out a blessing, that there shall not be room enough to receive it."

"Prove Me now," saith the LORD of hosts. Do it now and prove Him now! Do not wait; walk by faith and not by sight, and He will open the windows of heaven and pour you out a blessing. He will not sprinkle or dash you a blessing, but pour you out one, saith the LORD of hosts. You all will not have room enough to receive not only temporal but also spiritual blessings.

Verse 11: "And I will rebuke the devourer for your sakes, and he shall not destroy the fruits of your ground; neither shall your vine cast her fruit before the time in the field, saith the LORD of hosts."

The devourer is the devil. I Peter 5:8 declares, "Be sober, be vigilant; because your adversary the devil, as a roaring lion, walketh about, seeking whom he may devour." As I mentioned before, the devil wants you all to believe that what belongs to

Tithe and Tide

God is not imperative to return to Him. He deposits doubts in your mind to think that God understands you cannot give Him what He asked. "I have this and that to pay." So, you began to reason by saying if I return tithes and offerings, I will not be able to make ends meet. Therefore, you listen to the devil and take it upon yourselves to disobey God. The devil will laugh; he knows you will be cursed instead of blessed because of your rebellious spirit.

Verse 12: "And all nations shall call you blessed: for ye shall be a delightsome land, saith the LORD of hosts."

Verse 13: "Your words have been stout against Me, saith the LORD. Yet ye say, What have we spoken so much against Thee?"

Verse 14: "Ye have said, It is vain to serve God: and what profit is it that we have kept His ordinance, and that we have walked mournfully before the LORD of hosts?"

Verse 15: "And now we call the proud happy; yea, they that work wickedness are set up; yea, they that tempt God are even delivered."

Verse 16: "Then they that feared the LORD spake often one to another: and the LORD hearkened, and heard it, and a book of remembrance was written before Him for them that feared the LORD, and that thought upon His name."

Verse 17: "And they shall be Mine, saith the LORD of hosts, in that day when I make up My jewels; and I will spare them, as a man spareth his own son that serveth him."

Verse 18: "Then shall ye return, and discern between the righteous and the wicked, between him that serveth God and him that serveth Him not."

Just as Tide detergent cleanses our clothes, the tithe is used for the ministers to preach the gospel from the Word of God to cleanse us from within. Without the gospel of Christ, how can we be cleansed? Let us now prove that God and His Word can reach the people all over the world in which they too will have the privilege to hear, study, and submit to Him. They will be saved and cleansed from the inside out. May God bless you as you do His will by returning tithes and offerings; in return, He will rebuke the devourer for your sakes! Yes, God's only begotten Son is planning to descend from the clouds to escort His children home prepared for all of them who love and observe His powerful Word

CHAPTER 10

Scriptures to Consider for this Study

Luke 10:7; Leviticus 27:30, 32; Matthew 23:23; I Corinthians 9:13-14; Numbers 18:21; Proverbs 3:9.

According to *Webster's Dictionary*, 1828, the word tithe means, "The tenth part of anything; but appropriately, the tenth part of the increase annually arising from the profits of land and stock allotted to the clergy for their support. Tithes are personal, predial, or mixed; personal, when accruing from labor, art, trade, and navigation; predial, when issuing from the earth, as hay, wood and fruit; and mixed, when accruing from beasts, which are fed from the ground."

Additionally, from *Webster's Dictionary*, 1828, the word offering means, "That which is presented in divine service; an animal or a portion of bread or corn, or of gold and silver, or other valuable articles, presented to God as an atonement for sin, or as a return of thanks for His favors, or for other religious purposes; a sacrifice; an oblation." In our case, we have already received the atonement of Christ as our Lord and Savior.

Therefore, our offerings are presented to God "as a return of thanks for His favors, or for other religious purposes; a sacrifice; an oblation." Our offering keeps the church lights on, church expenses paid, and sometimes we may go beyond our regular offerings to God in making a sacrifice to help others in need.

An example of what a tenth is and what it looks like from your income: If you earned $100, your 10 percent is $10 and an offering of $5 or more or less, whatever God impresses you to give. A business owner cleared $5,000. After paying his employees, he has only $3,000 left from his profit. He returns 10 percent from the $3,000, which will be $300 and then an offering, maybe $150 or more or less, whatever he is prompted to contribute. Let your offering be given cheerfully because "God loveth a cheerful giver" (II Cor. 9:7).

Ten Percent Belongs to God and an Offering!

References

All Scriptures are from the *King James* Version (KJV) – public domain.

Webstersdictionary1828.com

www.ingramcontent.com/pod-product-compliance
Lightning Source LLC
LaVergne TN
LVHW021741060526
838200LV00052B/3398